"The fruit is already in the seed . . ."

ANO ANO
THE SEED

by

KRISTIN ZAMBUCKA

MANA PUBLISHING CO.
HONOLULU, HAWAII

Library of Congress Cataloging in Publication Data

Zambucka, Kristin.
    Ano ano: the seed.

    1. Spiritual life.   2. Mythology, Hawaiian.

I. Title.
BL624.Z35   1978   291.2   79-21424

Soft Cover ISBN 0-935038-00-0
Hard Cover ISBN 0-935038-01-9

All photographs by Alonzo Gartley
from the Bishop Museum collection.

© 1978 Copyright by KRISTIN ZAMBUCKA
First published March 1978
2nd printing October 1978
3rd printing October 1979
4th printing March 1981
5th printing November 1982
6th printing March 1984
7th printing June 1986

MANA PUBLISHING CO.
Honolulu, Hawaii 96813

INTRODUCTION

Mana is the life force itself emanating from a great universal source.

This sense of a higher power flowing through all living things; a force which could be harnessed by man for his own use, was the basic concept underlying all thought in preChristian Polynesia.

Dr. William Tufts Brigham, the first director of Honolulu's Bishop Museum, spent over forty years studying the kahuna of Hawaii with their astonishing ability to "harness the forces of nature and perform miracles." The Hawaiians had an effective prayer formula that consisted of planting a seed of thought and nourishing it daily with a gift of mana.

When the first company of Christian missionaries began preaching in Hawaii in 1820, they wielded a book magnificent in its content, but greatly misunderstood and misinterpreted. The well-meaning visitors translated its passages literally to the Islanders overlooking all of its truths veiled in symbolism and allegory.

A long period of painful confusion followed for the Hawaiian people. They were described as "heathens" for practicing their ancient rites, termed "immoral" for their liberal and healthy attitude towards sex and the life force and finally, during the 1890s, were forbidden to perform their "lewd and lascivious" hula (dance) which the Hawaiians themselves considered "an extension of the soul."

The visitors were ignorant of the teachings of the kahuna, of their multifaceted descriptions of human morality and of their instructions regarding the subtle differences involved in what they considered the greatest sin of all . . . the sin of hurting another.

The saddest feature of this conflict between the Hawaiians and the missionaries was that the Bible contained so many glimpses of similar teachings to what the Hawaiians had long been taught by their "Keepers of the Secret," the kahuna. Only the limited minds of the missionary interpreters got in the way of the merging of two enlightening paths to the one truth.

Sowing and reaping had long been a code for the Hawaiians. Of the many symbols used by the kahuna to veil their teachings, such as the "tree of life" and the "vine," the "seed" was the one most widely used.

So the Hawaiians took the Christian God, and gradually during the last 158 years, their beliefs came "full circle."

The mysteries of life were the same then as they are now . . . and human pain still seems without purpose, but insight provides hope. Although the kahuna trained in the old way have long since disappeared, the kahuna of today frequently use the Bible to solve human problems. All humanity is looking in the same direction, after all . . . but some are born to follow different paths.

After numerous years of research and painting throughout the Pacific area, I offer this volume as my own tribute, firstly to the Hawaiians whose images I borrowed to illustrate this book, and secondly to mankind's endless quest for a meaning to our existence.

Kristin Zambucka
Honolulu
Hawaii
Jan. 8, 1978

ANO ANO
THE SEED

Ageless coconut palms guarded the seekers' tryst against a backdrop of dark lofty mountains, scanned by a golden sickle of moon silently gleaming . . .

Androgynous in the shadows, they waited without faces or names, cooled by the scented leaves that brushed against them.

Three of the older ones rested with their bodies stretched out face down so they could smell the damp earth.

Like sphinxes their backs arched as they raised their heads taking the weight on their outstretched forearms.

In the moonlight they became dignified effigies in stone . . . monuments to their old selves.

Their aura grew tense and vulnerable as they inhaled the fragrant night . . . and examined their feelings.

At last the stage was set for truth.

Long had they searched and far, in seemingly endless circles outside themselves, for a meaning to their existence.

The time had come for answers as their journey took a new turn . . . inward.

"And what of life? Why are we here at all?" they asked.
And the old ones answered, too simply, that life is a series of lessons
to be learned.
"But why all the suffering that haunts us throughout our years?"
they questioned.
"We didn't ask to be born. Why must we pay such a price for this
consciousness?"

"You were never born," they were told. "You can never die, so you were never born. Know that you ARE. Life is an endless chain of experiences as we grow spiritually back towards our source. Take charge of your consciousness.
Sowing and reaping is all you need to practice.
Plant well your good seeds and pluck up the bad."

"We are all on a spiral path.
No growth takes place in a straight line.
There will be setbacks along the way . . .
There will be shadows, but they will be balanced by patches of light
and fountains of joy as we grow and progress.
Awareness of the pattern is all you need to sustain you along the
way . . ."

"Kumulaʻau — the tree"

"We all live many lives.
Even during our present span of days and nights . . . we may act out
many roles.
We have all been all things, so never condemn another for what he
may be.
Our circumstances may change . . . problems are presented . . .
and complexes long buried may rise to the surface of the mind.
Some are hangovers from an endless past of struggles for survival."

"Know that there is a path to a higher consciousness within ourselves . . .
and you alone are the keeper of that path . . . a path that can be blocked by the events of life.
Make amends for the wrong you have done to others and rid yourselves of guilt.
Free yourselves from feelings of injustice . . . and injustice will no longer stalk you.
Your suffering is only caused by your thoughts.
You are in charge of your mind . . . free it.
No difficulty has any power over you unless you give it that power.
Let past events fade away
and don't allow them to paint dark colors on your future."

"And when the paralyzing ache of despair engulfs you, and you reel shaken from the blows that life deals you, and you scream out, demanding to know what you've done to deserve it . . .
And when you know that you can't take any more but it strikes you again, harder this time, from another side, and you are just hanging on by a thread until you feel yourself curl inward and die a little . . .
Know that there is a reason for it all . . ."

The old ones went on to explain the meaning of life itself . . .
and they gave the listeners hope.
"We are not here for nothing," they said. "Life is not just a bad joke.
Suffering unlocks the door to many answers and fire purifies.
If you look back and examine some pain of the past, you will see
that it taught you so much that no other teacher could . . .
Only when wounded do we stand still and listen.
Bleeding, you will be brought to your knees many times.
But somehow, nourished by an indomitable thread of strength
within . . . you will go on.
Your eyes will not really see until they are incapable of tears.
Only when you can cry no more will you begin to grow."

"The salute to mana"

"It is then that you will hear a voice within yourself.
It was there all the time, but you never listened before.
Faintly it will speak to you at first, but it will gradually grow louder
and clearer the more you take heed of its message
until one day it thunders inside you and you will have come home."

And listening . . . listening, they came to rely on its judgment. They made fewer mistakes as closing their eyes, ignoring appearances, they "saw" with that voice within and learned to trust it, as it was the nearest they came to hearing the voice of God.

". . . and the tree was barren."

Spirit alone is immortal.
Man is made up of ideas . . . and ideas will guide his life.
The physical body is lent to us so that spirit may come into contact with matter.
Neither worship that body nor neglect it . . . but respect the instrument you have been given to pursue this earthly life.

We are all children of the one father.
The same essence of life dwells in all of us . . . to protect and
nourish; to heal and to guide.
If we turn to it and trust it, we will not be turned away.
Once you find this presence you will rest secure.
You can then be a father to someone else.

"The presence within is the true
father of man.
And all that the father has is
already yours . . .
For you and the father are one . . ."

Children do not remain children forever, but move through various stages towards maturity.
And so it is with consciousness.
We outgrow people, places and things as we unfold.
We shed the old self to make way for the new self to be born.
There is no death, but a constant cycle of rebirth . . .
An endless chain as we grow towards spiritual perfection.

And for long hours they recited flowery words of praise to this benevolent friend they had found . . .
this ancient patriarch with the long white beard and the powers of a magician who would dissolve their troubles with a wave of his hand and set things right for them.
But still their prayers went unheard . . .
and they lamented the deaf ears of God who heard them not.

And seeing their dilemma the old ones described for the listeners the most sacred truth of all . . .
The very nature of the presence they must call God. . . and for some strange reason, describe as a man.
"Eradicate all thoughts about the appearance of this being," they said, "for you can never know God with your mind.
Cease thinking of God and begin sensing and feeling his oneness with yourself. . . then he will exist.
Never was God outside yourself or separate from you.
We need only be receptive and the substance of his power will flow through us.
We are really but instruments and we will be used.
It is only through our consciousness that God can enter this world.
He then translates into our human experience.
The blessing will manifest in the form of material advantages . . . a bearing of fruit."

And the night was still as they were given the greatest gift that mankind can receive . . . the formula for having their prayers answered.
But there was one essential condition to observe:
Would the prayer hurt someone else?
For the only real "sin" to them was in hurting another's feelings or coveting his material possessions.

"Enter the realms
of mystery and spirit
and find your reality . . ."

HO'ANO
[Making The Seed]

Form a clear unwavering picture in your mind . . . of the condition
or object you desire.
Be very careful of the details of your picture for the subconscious
mind that will receive it is sharply accurate . . .
and you will get the exact replica of what you envisage.
Forget the old condition entirely . . . let it fall away from your
mind.
Clearly see the new desired state.
Paint the picture carefully inside your head . . . and resist any
changing of your mind.
Act then as if you had already received the condition for which you
asked.
Feel it already upon you with the love or joy or whatever emotion
you would experience if it were so.
Act it out.
For this subconscious mind of which we speak . . . this unihipili
. . . is like a child.
It loves pictures and will respond also to any emotional surge you
project to it.
Daily thereafter gather mana by taking four deep breaths and offer
it as a gift to the God within you.
Then after this offering each day, recall the "seed picture" of your
desire and offer it anew also . . . to the same higher consciousness
within yourself.
This practice will strengthen the picture and make it clearer as it
nears the stage where it will take form.
Until your seed bears its fruit . . . hold it close to you as a secret . . .
for any mention of its contents to another will spill its power to
reach fruition.
Wash out all your doubts . . . they can so discourage the subconscious
that the daily rite will be interrupted and your fruit will "wither on
the vine."

And the truth of it shook them as they wandered awestruck in the shadow of the mountain.

WE CREATE GOD.

And the voice inside them thundered:

IF YOU BELIEVE IN ME . . . I AM.

The impact of their discovery was too great and too simple to believe at first.

How could the object of their long quest be so close at hand?

And they doubted and were distressed at the deceit of the voice they were learning to trust.

And the old ones saw their confusion and instructed them to accept the presence within and to nourish it with words and thoughts and offerings of mana.

So they talked to this presence that dwelt within.

And they knew at last the peace of answered prayers.

And the hand of the father rested on them.

"Do not condemn your days," the old ones said.
"Stop the battle within and strive to understand yourself instead.
Live well this life . . . plant good seeds . . . find the presence of God
within and seek its help."
The next life and the life before this one were of little interest to the
people of old.
But the more they pondered the seeming futility of this incarnation
with all its pain and disappointment . . . they were prompted to ask:
"And what of former lives?"
And the old ones answered:
"There is no real remembrance. A memory here . . . a vision there
. . . but you will not know who you once were or whom you may yet
become."

*"And all the days of your
life you will seek mana . . ."*

*And they were taught the laws of life . . . that their treatment of
others would return at last upon themselves.
Those who cheat will be cheated.
Those who slander will be slandered.
For every lie you tell . . . you will be lied to.
Brutality will meet with brutality.
We get what we give and to the same degree.
And not always from the same people with whom we've dealt.
But somewhere . . . sometime . . . someone will treat you in like
manner.
The good that we do to others will return also.
For your kindness to strangers you will receive hospitality in far
places yourself.
Understand the troubles of others who come to you with their souls
bared . . . and when you cry yourself, you will be sympathetically
understood.
We get what we give.
Like always attracts like.
This is the law and it is inevitable.
We cannot escape the results of our actions.*

Security takes root only in your state of mind.
Why seek the approval of others?
You tried to make them like you, but the feeling of comfort you
sought did not come.
And the old ones understood . . .
"You will find no security in acting that way," they said.
"Anxiety will soon cramp you again like the chill of dawn,
and you will have forfeited your integrity."

"Mana — the water
of life."

We outgrow people, places, and things as we unfold.
We may be saddened when old friends say their piece and leave our
lives . . . but let them go.
They were at a different stage . . . looking in a different direction.
They stood still while you advanced in your thoughts and
aspirations and the friendship was strained for a long time,
but neither party had the heart to let it go.
Remember we have no duty to drag them along with us as we grow.
There is nothing to give each other any more . . .
and one day you see a stranger behind the other's eyes,
eyes you once thought you knew.

Each life has its own special design.
We only acquire and keep what truly belongs to us.
There is trouble if we try to take what is not ours or what is not right
for our development.
Sometimes we are violently pitchforked away from someone or
something that we have wanted.
And we rage against the stroke of fate that breaks up the alliance.
But it may have been disastrous had we stayed.
If we look back at the remade situation,
all evens out and harmony is restored in the end.
We find our right place at the right time and with the right person.

"The Androgynes"

And if your spirit does not rest easily inside you,
if you yearn for another form,
it may be a hangover from a former life . . .
a shadow of someone you once were.
We bring strange yearnings with us on our journey from the past,
for somewhere along the line, we have been all things . . .
man and woman . . . beggar and merchant . . . pauper and
potentate.
Though mankind is only one, it wears a million masks.
There is a secret life in nature
where both male and female can exist in the same plant . . .
and have we not been told that man's earthly predecessor was an
androgyne?

*For mana is the silent force permeating all of nature . . .
the magnificent energy flowing through all living things.
It can be harnessed and gathered by man to increase his own
power . . . if only he can find its source.
All living matter is modeled by it.
And we spend our whole lives seeking it as a holy quest . . .
and our hearts will find no peace until they rest in it,
for it flows from the supreme being we call God.
Once found, the whole world takes on a new splendour.
It becomes a thing of mysterious and sacred significance.
The seed of all things lies buried within us until the gift of mana is
offered to it.
A seed regenerates and never dies.
It sprouts and grows again . . .
and life continues in a never ending cycle.
All our strength and power lies in finding our source of mana.
If we truly find it and recognize its source, it will never cease to flow.
It is an endless channel of blessings.*

Pain accompanies all birth.
There is pain when we are born . . .
and there is pain when we are re-born
as old facets of the personality die away . . .
or are brutally torn out of our life pattern . . . to make way for the
new.
In breaking down the old future, one's world may seem to fall
apart.
Trouble will enter the life like a storm . . .
A tempest will rage.
Do not resist . . .
there is a balancing power at work . . .
for your new self is about to enter the world.

Though I may travel far I will meet only what I carry with me,
for every man is a mirror.
We see only ourselves reflected in those around us.
Their attitudes and actions are reflections of our own.
The whole world and its conditions has its counterpart within us
all.
Turn the gaze inward . . .
correct yourself and your world will change.

Forgive yourself for past mistakes.
Let them go from your mind . . . the only place they ever were . . .
hanging on like gnawing aches that spoil your present experience of
life.
Stop imposing the agony of remorse on yourself,
and see yourself acting back then as a child . . . without insight
. . . without maturity.
You have grown since.
The mistakes contributed to that growth.
You would not act the same way now.
You cannot change the past . . . but you can change your thoughts
about it.
An attitude is ours to control.
We are the creators.
Change your thoughts and you change your world.

Life is full of change.
The good passes . . . but so does the bad.
Nothing remains the same in this unstable world.
Not a single element of anything . . . physical or mental . . . is the same today as it was yesterday.
When we are down at the bottom of the pit of despair . . . the only way to go is up.
If we only wait a little . . . the cycle . . . the endless unfailing tide of things will sweep us up again.
"Without darkness," said the old ones, "we would not appreciate the light when it comes."

What then do we owe to others?
And they were told that we owe them nothing
except to grow mature ourselves . . . to find the real self within us
all.
You cannot help anyone . . .
but you can be the friend that they always hoped existed.
BE something for them.
Out of their own confusion others may try to dictate our duties to us.
Drop such burdens.
We cannot love those we feel it our duty to love.
Face the reality of the person's makeup.
We owe him nothing if his personality repels our love or kindness.
We must all earn the right to be loved.
And do not expect love
if you are incapable of giving it.

"And at last
their bonds were
broken . . ."

Long will you wander in a wilderness of confusion and distress until you come home . . . to a higher consciousness.
Know that all your development will take place in silence.
Much of your growth will be caused by shocks,
but your real evolution of spirit will be a silent process.
Your new consciousness will manifest in your surroundings.
As you elevate, so will your setting in life improve.
You may hide and take refuge in the house you have built in silence . . . the sanctuary within.

"You can have everything if you only know how to ask.
The essence of the desired object is already within yourself.
Be aware that the fruit is already in the seed.
Formulate your images and ask.
Your seed of thought will bud, blossom and bear fruit.
Everything that happens to us is the result of a seed once planted.
Our present experience is the result of past decisions . . .
change your mind today,
and you build your world of tomorrow.
Your mind is your garden . . . tend it well," they said.

And what of the hereafter? What is beyond this life?
The old ones would soon long for sleep and they whispered,
"We go back whence we came.
All is spirit in the end.
We take nothing with us.
The body falls back into the earth and the spirit, rich or poor,
lives on.
We all live forever . . . somewhere."